CONTENTS

THE DEVIL'S TRIANGLE

There is an area in the Atlantic Ocean, east of the United States, that has been the site of many strange incidents. In this area, planes have disappeared from radar screens and ships have turned up with no crew. All these mysteries seem to have one thing in common – nobody has been able to solve them.

WHAT'S IN A NAME?

This area is known by many names, such as the Devil's Triangle and Hoodoo Sea. Most famously, it is called The Bermuda Triangle. On a map, it can be roughly marked out as a triangle that stretches from Miami, Florida, to Puerto Rico, to Bermuda, and back to Miami. The influence of this mysterious stretch of ocean, however, can often make itself felt outside its boundaries.

STRANGE FORCES

Although many of the planes and ships have disappeared without a trace, some of the people involved have lived to report their terrifying experiences (see page 38). Others have left recordings taken during radio communications, before disappearing. These records tell of compasses going haywire, strange fogs in which the sea and the sky blend together, and sightings of unidentified flying objects (UFOs). In 1980, pilots José Torres and José Santos were flying back to Puerto Rico from the Dominican Republic when their radio transmissions indicated that they were trying to avoid a UFO. They were never seen again. In this, and in many other cases, it is as if the plane, or boat, and its entire crew have disappeared!

THE BERMUDA TRIANGLE

STRANGE OCCURRENCES AT SEA

by David West

illustrated by Mike Lacey

BOOK HOUSE

Designed and produced by
David West ♞ Children's Books
7 Princeton Court
55 Felsham Road
London SW15 1AZ

Editor: Dominique Crowley

Photo credits:
Page 6 (bottom left), 6/7 – U.S. Air Force
Page 7 (top) – Fate Magazine.
Pages 44/45 – NOAA

First published in 2006 by **Book House,**
an imprint of **The Salariya Book Company Ltd**
25 Marlborough Place, Brighton BN1 1UB

The Salariya
BOOK CO. Ltd

Please visit the Salariya Book Company at:
www.salariya.com

HB ISBN 1 905087 63 2
PB ISBN 1 905087 64 0

Visit our website at **www.book-house.co.uk**
for free electronic versions of:
You Wouldn't Want to Be an Egyptian Mummy!
You Wouldn't Want to Be a Roman Gladiator!
Avoid joining Shackleton's Polar Expedition!

A catalogue record for this book is available from the British Library.

Printed on paper from sustainable forests.

Manufactured in China.

ATLANTIC OCEAN

•Cape Hatteras
•Cape Lookout
•Cape Fear

NORTH
AMERICA

FLORIDA

•Last reported
position of Flight 19

THE

BERMUDA

TRIANGLE

•Fort Lauderdale

Key
West •Miami   BAHAMAS

Florida
Keys

CUBA

HAITI DOMINICAN
        REPUBLIC

PUERTO
RICO

CARIBBEAN SEA

SOUTH
AMERICA

BERMUDA

N

W   E

S

THE ORIGINS OF THE BERMUDA TRIANGLE

GRAPHIC MYSTERIES — THE BERMUDA TRIANGLE

On the morning of January 30, 1948, a BSAAC Tudor IV airliner, *Star Tiger*, suddenly disappeared less than two hours from its destination – Bermuda!

UNSOLVED MYSTERY

A thorough investigation led to a report that concluded "...the fate of *Star Tiger* must remain an unsolved mystery." Almost a year later on January 17, 1949, another BSAAC Tudor IV airliner, *Star Ariel*, took off from Bermuda, bound for Jamaica, and was never heard from again! 20 days earlier a *DC3* airliner (Flight NC16002) was approaching Miami International Airport with 31 passengers and crew on board. The pilot radioed in to say that he was only 80 km out.

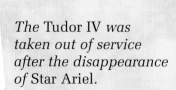

The Tudor IV *was taken out of service after the disappearance of* Star Ariel.

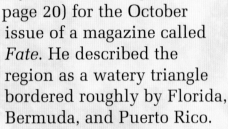

That was the last that was ever heard or seen of the plane. The area where it disappeared has shallow seas, so wrecks would have been easy to see. Nothing was discovered in the search that followed.

THE TRIANGLE

It was these unexplained disappearances that alerted people to this mysterious section of ocean. In 1952, journalist George Sand wrote an article about these mysteries and Flight 19 (see page 20) for the October issue of a magazine called *Fate*. He described the region as a watery triangle bordered roughly by Florida, Bermuda, and Puerto Rico.

Designed in 1935, the DC3 was a robust plane that became the world's most successful airliner.

DEADLY

On February 3, 1963, the *S.S. Marine Sulphur Queen* mysteriously disappeared off Florida's south coast. Her last message placed her near Key West. Neither the ship nor her 39 crew members were ever found. A year later, an article about this mystery appeared in the *Argosy* magazine by a journalist whose name was Vincent Gaddis.

BERMUDA

Newspaper articles and magazine stories appeared using various names for the area. But it was not until 1972 that Charles Berlitz coined the term 'The Bermuda Triangle' in his book of the same name. The book was a runaway bestseller.

THE MYSTERIOUS CASE OF THE DESERTED SCHOONER THE *CARROLL A. DEERING*

AUGUST 1920, NORFOLK, VIRGINIA. THE CARROLL A. DEERING IS BEING LOADED WITH COAL. SHE IS BOUND FOR RIO DE JANEIRO, BRAZIL. THE CAPTAIN, WILLIAM M. MERRITT, IS SIGNING ON THE CREW. HE HAS ALREADY SIGNED ON HIS SON, S.E. MERRITT, AS FIRST MATE.

JOHAN FREDRICKSON OF FINLAND, AGE 48, HEIGHT — 1.70 METRES, COMPLEXION — RUDDY, HAIR — SAME, SIGN HERE.

LATER THE SAME MONTH, THE SCHOONER SETS SAIL.

SHORTLY AFTERWARDS, THE CAPTAIN BECOMES ILL. THE SHIP HAS TO STOP AT LEWES, DELAWARE.

IT'S QUITE SERIOUS. I'M AFRAID HE CANNOT CONTINUE WITH THIS VOYAGE.

MERRITT IS TAKEN ASHORE WITH HIS SON, LEAVING THE SHIP WITHOUT A CAPTAIN AND FIRST MATE.

THE DEERING COMPANY FINDS A NEW CAPTAIN. HIS NAME IS WILLIS B. WORMELL. HIS FIRST TASK IS TO FIND A FIRST MATE. HE HIRES CHARLES B. MCLELLAN.

STOW YOUR GEAR BELOW. WE'LL BE CASTING OFF WITH THE NEXT TIDE.

AYE, HUMPH...

FINALLY, ON SEPTEMBER 8, THE CARROLL A. DEERING SETS SAIL FOR RIO.

THE SCHOONER ARRIVES IN RIO AND UNLOADS HER CARGO. THE CREW HAVE A FEW DAYS OF SHORE LEAVE TO ENJOY IN THE CITY.

CAPTAIN WORMELL VISITS CAPTAIN GOODWIN, AN OLD FRIEND.

HOW WONDERFUL IT IS TO SEE YOU, WILLIS. HOW WAS YOUR TRIP?

IT WAS TOLERABLE. BUT MY FIRST MATE IS A WORTHLESS TROUBLEMAKER.

FORTUNATELY THOUGH, MY ENGINEER, HERBERT BATES, IS QUITE RELIABLE.

AH, YES. I KNOW THE MAN WELL.

DECEMBER 2, 1920, THE CARROLL A. DEERING SETS SAIL FOR HOME.

10

THE SHIP STOPS AT BARBADOS IN THE CARIBBEAN FOR SUPPLIES. ONCE AGAIN, THE CREW IS GIVEN SOME FREE TIME TO SPEND ON THE ISLAND.

CAPTAIN, MCLELLAN HAS BEEN ARRESTED AND JAILED FOR BEING DRUNK IN PUBLIC.

CAPTAIN WORMELL USES HIS AUTHORITY TO GET MCLELLAN RELEASED JUST BEFORE THEY SAIL. BUT FOR SOME UNKNOWN REASON, MCLELLAN IS UNHAPPY...

THANK YOU, OFFICER. I'LL MAKE SURE HE GIVES YOU NO MORE TROUBLE.

ARRGG! YAH STUCK UP FOOL. I'LL KILL YAH, SO I WILL!

JANUARY 9, 1921, THE CARROLL A. DEERING SETS OUT ON ITS RETURN TRIP TO NORFOLK.

RROLL A. DEE

BATH

THE CARROLL A. DEERING GLIDES ON INTO THE DISTANCE, HEADING ALONG THE COAST.

SHORTLY AFTERWARD, A STEAMER PASSES BY. JACOBSON, THE LIGHTSHIP KEEPER, WHO SPOKE TO THE MEN ABOUT THE DEERING, DECIDES TO HAIL IT AND ASK ITS CAPTAIN TO PASS ON THE MESSAGE FROM THE CARROLL A. DEERING.

PAAAARP

ALTHOUGH ALL SHIPS MUST RESPOND TO A LIGHTSHIP'S HORN, THE STEAMER CARRIES ON.

HMMM...THE SHIP'S NAME IS COVERED. SHE'S PROBABLY A RUM RUNNER.

FEBRUARY 4, THE COAST GUARD CUTTER, THE *MANNING*, SENDS A BOARDING PARTY TO A SCHOONER THAT IS STUCK FAST ON DIAMOND SHOALS, NEAR CAPE HATTERAS, NORTH CAROLINA. IT IS DUE WEST OF THE BERMUDA TRIANGLE'S NORTHERN TIP.

CAN YOU SEE HER NAME?

IT'S THE *CARROLL A. DEERING*, SIR.

HER SAILS ARE ALL SET FOR SAILING, BUT THE LIFEBOATS ARE GONE.

10:30 A.M.

AHOY THERE!

WHERE IS EVERYONE?

AHOY THERE! IS THERE ANYONE ABOARD?

THAT'S STRANGE, THERE IS FOOD PREPARED, READY TO COOK A MEAL.

SIR, THERE'S NO SIGN OF THE SHIP'S PAPERS OR NAVIGATION INSTRUMENTS.

SHE'S COMPLETELY DESERTED! HELLO, WHAT HAVE WE GOT HERE?

IN THE CAPTAIN'S CABIN, THEY FIND A MAP RECORDING THE SHIP'S MOVEMENTS.

LOOK! THE HANDWRITING IS DIFFERENT HERE. AND THIS ENTRY IS DIFFERENT FROM BOTH OF THE OTHERS. WE BETTER TAKE THIS WITH US.

ALL THE CREW'S GEAR IS MISSING. IT DOESN'T MAKE SENSE. IF THEY ABANDONED SHIP, WHY DIDN'T THEY HEAD FOR THE COAST?

LOOK! SOMEONE HUNG RED LIGHTS ON THE MASTS.*

*RED LIGHTS HUNG ON THE MASTS MEANS THE SHIP IS DERELICT, OR OUT OF CONTROL.

4:30 P.M.

WE'LL SEE IF WE CAN TOW HER AWAY FROM THESE SHOALS. SHE CAN'T BE LEFT HERE AS A DANGER TO OTHER SHIPS.

THE CARROLL A. DEERING CANNOT BE MOVED. JUST A MONTH LATER, HOWEVER, ON MARCH 4, SHE IS DELIBERATELY BLOWN UP.

KABOOM

THE STRANGE CIRCUMSTANCES IN WHICH THE *CARROLL A. DEERING* WAS FOUND DEMAND AN INVESTIGATION. THE U.S. GOVERNMENT HAS FIVE SEPARATE DEPARTMENTS LOOKING INTO THE CASE. THE MAN IN CHARGE IS LAWRENCE RICHEY.

THAT'S ONLY FOUR DAYS BEFORE THE LIGHTSHIP SIGHTED THE *CARROLL A. DEERING.*

THERE'S SOMETHING YOU SHOULD KNOW, MR. RICHEY. ANOTHER SHIP HAS GONE MISSING. THE *S.S. HEWITT* DISAPPEARED ON JANUARY 25, VERY CLOSE TO WHERE THE CARROLL WAS FOUND.

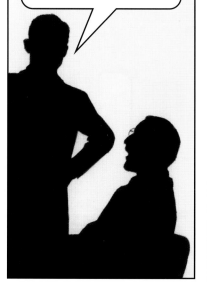

THE STEAMER WITH HER NAME COVERED, SPOTTED SOON AFTER THE CARROLL WAS MET BY THE LIGHTSHIP, COULD HAVE BEEN A PIRATE SHIP. MAYBE THEY ATTACKED BOTH SHIPS?

"THE PIRATES COULD HAVE SUNK THE HEWITT AND THEN ATTACKED THE CARROLL!"

NO, I DON'T THINK SO. THERE WAS NO SIGN OF A STRUGGLE.

"I THINK MCLELLAN WAS RESPONSIBLE. REMEMBER, HE THREATENED CAPTAIN WORMELL'S LIFE."

"THE MAP SHOWS THAT WORMELL'S HANDWRITING STOPS ON JANUARY 23, EIGHT DAYS BEFORE THE SHIP RAN AGROUND. I BELIEVE THE CAPTAIN WAS KILLED BY MCLELLAN."

"MCLELLAN PROBABLY HELD THE REST OF THE CREW PRISONER AT GUNPOINT. HE NEEDED THEM ALIVE, SINCE HE COULDN'T SAIL THE BOAT ON HIS OWN."

18

"WHEN THE LIGHTSHIP KEEPER SAW THEM, THEY WERE ON THE POOP DECK, USUALLY RESERVED FOR OFFICERS ONLY. I THINK MCLELLAN WAS OUT OF SIGHT, COVERING THEM WITH A GUN."

"THEN, I THINK HE FORCED THE CREW INTO BOATS AND SET THE SHIP TO RUN AGROUND ON THE SHOALS, BEFORE GETTING INTO HIS OWN LIFEBOAT WITH THE SHIP'S PAPERS."

"THAT'S ONLY MY OPINION. BUT WHAT I CAN'T WORK OUT IS WHAT HAPPENED TO THE CREW. WHAT HAPPENED TO MCLELLAN? WHERE DID THEY GO? IT SEEMS LIKE THEY DISAPPEARED INTO THE WATERY WASTES. PERHAPS IT WILL ALWAYS REMAIN A MYSTERY."

THE END

FLIGHT 19 'THE LOST PATROL'

I'LL BE RELIEVED WHEN THIS ONE'S OVER.

YEAH, ME TOO, POWERS. I'M GLAD THIS IS THE LAST TEST.

DECEMBER 5, 1945, 1 P.M., NAVAL AIR STATION (NAS) FORT LAUDERDALE, FLORIDA, AT THE WESTERN EDGE OF THE BERMUDA TRIANGLE. CAPTAIN E.J. POWERS WALKS TOWARD THE TRAINING OFFICE WITH OTHER MEMBERS OF FLIGHT 19. THEY ARE ABOUT TO BE BRIEFED ON THEIR THIRD, AND FINAL, NAVIGATION TEST.

MECHANICS GIVE THE FIVE GRUMMAN AVENGERS OF FLIGHT 19 A FINAL CHECK.

OK, ALL THE SURVIVAL GEAR IS ON BOARD. FUEL TANKS ARE FULL. ALL INSTRUMENTS HAVE BEEN CHECKED.

HEY, JOE, HOW COME NONE OF THE PLANES HAS A CLOCK?

'CAUSE EVERY SOUVENIR HUNTER THIS SIDE OF THE ATLANTIC WANTS ONE. IF WE PUT CLOCKS IN THE COCKPIT, THEY'D GET STOLEN AS QUICK AS YOU COULD SAY "WHAT TIME IS IT?"

BUT HOW ARE THE PILOTS GOING TO NAVIGATE WITHOUT CLOCKS?

HEY, DON'T WORRY ABOUT IT. THEY'LL BE WEARING THEIR WRISTWATCHES.

1315 HOURS (1:15 P.M.). LIEUTENANT CHARLES TAYLOR, THE INSTRUCTOR FOR FLIGHT 19, ARRIVES AT THE TRAINING DUTY OFFICE. HE IS A COMBAT VETERAN WITH MORE THAN 2,500 HOURS OF FLYING TIME.

LISTEN, CAN YOU FIND ANOTHER INSTRUCTOR TO TAKE THIS FLIGHT?

IT'S A BIT LATE FOR THAT. THE FLIGHT'S DUE TO TAKE OFF AT 1345 HOURS (1:45 P.M.). WHY?

I JUST DON'T WANT TO TAKE THIS ONE OUT.

I'M SORRY. THERE'S NO ONE ELSE TO REPLACE YOU.

MUTTER
MUTTER
MUTTER

BRIEFING ROOM

NAVIGATION PROBLEM NUMBER ONE IS AS FOLLOWS: ONE: DEPART NAS FORT LAUDERDALE AND FLY 091 DEGREES, FOR 90 KM TO HENS AND CHICKEN SHOALS TO CONDUCT LOW LEVEL BOMBING AND, AFTER BOMBING, CONTINUE ON COURSE 091 FOR 107 KM. TWO: FLY COURSE 346 DEGREES FOR 117 KM. THREE: FLY COURSE 241 DEGREES FOR 193 KM, RETURNING TO NAS FORT LAUDERDALE. THIS AFTERNOON, THE WEATHER IS FAVOURABLE WITH MODERATE TO ROUGH SEAS...

GENTLEMEN, I AM LIEUTENANT TAYLOR. I WILL BE YOUR INSTRUCTOR FOR TODAY.

POWERS, YOU TAKE THE LEAD. I'LL BRING UP THE REAR TO KEEP AN EYE ON THE FLIGHT.

1410 HOURS (2:10 P.M.). THE FIVE GRUMMAN AVENGERS OF FLIGHT 19 ARE AIRBORNE.

1439 HOURS (2:39 P.M.). FLIGHT 19 ARRIVES AT HENS AND CHICKEN SHOALS. THEY SPEND 30 MINUTES ON BOMBING PRACTICE.

FOX TARE TWO EIGHT, THIS IS FOX TARE THREE SIX. I'VE GOT ONE MORE BOMB...

...GO AHEAD AND DROP IT.

WHHEeeeee

KERBOOM

1500 HOURS (3:00 P.M.). A FISHING BOAT CAPTAIN, WORKING NEAR THE TARGET AREA, SEES PLANES FLYING EAST.

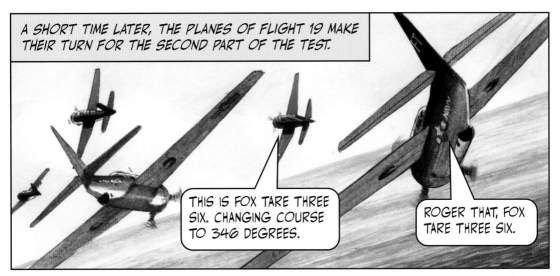

A SHORT TIME LATER, THE PLANES OF FLIGHT 19 MAKE THEIR TURN FOR THE SECOND PART OF THE TEST.

THIS IS FOX TARE THREE SIX. CHANGING COURSE TO 346 DEGREES.

ROGER THAT, FOX TARE THREE SIX.

1540 HOURS (3:40 P.M.).

WHAT THE...?

POWERS, WHAT DOES YOUR COMPASS READ?

TAP TAP

ABOVE THE AIRFIELD AT FORT LAUDERDALE, THE SENIOR FLIGHT INSTRUCTOR, LIEUTENANT ROBERT COX, PICKS UP VOICES ON HIS RADIO.

WHAT DOES IT READ NOW? TSCHH.. POWERS, WHAT DOES YOUR COMPASS READ NOW?

*A CHAIN OF ISLANDS RUNNING SOUTHWEST FROM THE FLORIDA PENINSULA AND LYING JUST A FEW KILOMETRES FROM THE SOUTHWESTERN POINT OF THE BERMUDA TRIANGLE.

29

FT-74

ROGER THAT. TURN ON YOUR EMERGENCY IFF.*

*IDENTIFICATION FRIEND OR FOE

1626 HOURS (4:26 P.M.). AIR-SEA RESCUE TASK UNIT FOUR (ASRTU-4) AT FORT EVERGLADES HEARS FT-28.

I AM AT ANGELS THREE FIVE. HAVE ON EMERGENCY IFF. DOES ANYONE IN THE AREA HAVE A RADAR SCREEN THAT COULD PICK US UP?

ROGER THAT, FOX TARE TWO EIGHT.

SINCE ASRTU-4 HAS NO DIRECTION-FINDER, THEY CONTACT NAS FORT LAUDERDALE, WHO CONTACT NAS MIAMI AND OTHER STATIONS THAT HAVE DIRECTION-FINDERS OR RADAR.

MORE THAN 20 STATIONS ARE NOW LOOKING FOR FLIGHT 19. SO ARE SHIPS IN THE AREA.

ANY LUCK?

NO. WE'RE GETTING LOTS OF INTERFERENCE FROM CUBAN RADIO STATIONS.

LIEUTENANT COX LANDS FT-74 BACK AT NAS FORT LAUDERDALE.

THIS IS FOX TARE SEVEN FOUR, RETURNING TO BASE.

HE TELLS THE DUTY OFFICER EVERYTHING THAT HAS HAPPENED, THEN GOES TO SEE THE FLIGHT OFFICER.

REQUEST PERMISSION TO CONTINUE THE SEARCH FOR FLIGHT 19, SIR.

SORRY, LIEUTENANT. IT'S TOO RISKY WITH NIGHT APPROACHING, AND BAD WEATHER IS MOVING THIS WAY FROM PALM BEACH.

1645 HOURS (4:45 P.M.). FT-28 IS HEARD BY ASRTU-4.

WE ARE HEADING 030 DEGREES FOR 45 MINUTES, THEN WE WILL FLY NORTH TO MAKE SURE WE ARE NOT OVER THE GULF OF MEXICO.

FOX TARE TWO EIGHT, SWITCH TO 3,000KC. I SAY AGAIN, SWITCH TO 3,000KC, OVER.*

* THE SEARCH AND RESCUE FREQUENCY.

FT-28

I CANNOT SWITCH FREQUENCIES. I MUST KEEP IN CONTACT WITH MY PLANES.

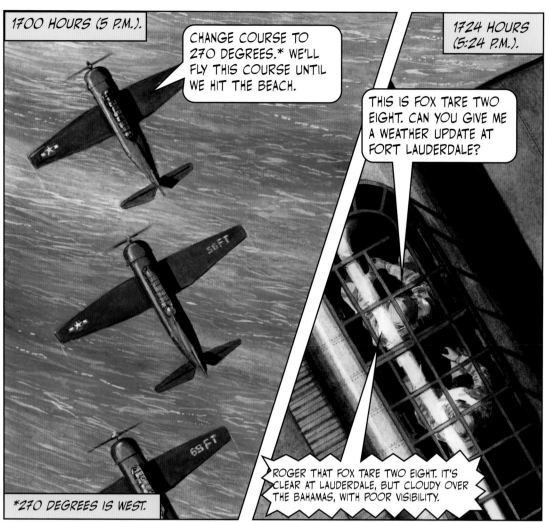

1804 HOURS (6:04 P.M.). FT-28

WHERE ARE WE? IF WE ARE IN THE GULF OF MEXICO, WE SHOULD HEAD NORTH OR EAST. WE'RE RUNNING LOW ON FUEL.

HOLDING COURSE 270 DEGREES. WE DIDN'T GO FAR ENOUGH EAST... WE MAY AS WELL JUST TURN AROUND AND GO EAST AGAIN.

MEANWHILE, IN FORT LAUDERDALE...

GOOD NEWS, SIR! WE'VE GOT A RELIABLE FIX ON THEIR LOCATION! THEY'RE WITHIN A HUNDRED-KILOMETRE RADIUS OF 029 DEGREES NORTH, 079 DEGREES WEST.

TWO PBM-5 SEAPLANES ARE SENT TO THE AREA.

BUT THAT PUTS THEM NORTHEAST OF HERE. THEY'RE OVER THE BERMUDA TRIANGLE!

During the search for Flight 19, a PBM-5 catches fire and is seen to explode at sea at 7:50 P.M. with the loss of all 13 crew members. No wreckage is found. Hundreds of ships and aircraft cover 518,000 square km of ocean. The search for Flight 19 continues for five days, before being called off. No wreckage or lifejackets are ever found. The Navy board of inquiry can make no sense of the complete disappearance of Flight 19.

THE END

CAPTAIN HENRY AND THE MAGNETIC FOG

1966. MID-AFTERNOON ON BOARD THE TUG, *THE GOOD NEWS,* THREE DAYS OUT FROM PUERTO RICO HEADING FOR MIAMI. THE TUG IS TOWING AN EMPTY BARGE WEIGHING 2,540 TONNES, WITH A 182-METRE TOW-ROPE, ON A CALM SEA..

CHUGGA CHUG CHUGGA CHUG

CAPTAIN DON HENRY IS IN HIS CABIN WHEN HE HEARS SHOUTS COMING FROM THE BRIDGE.

WHAT THE...?

HE RUSHES UP TO THE WHEELHOUSE.

WHAT'S GOING ON HERE?

TAKE A LOOK AT THE COMPASS, CAP.

WHAT ON EARTH...?

I'VE NEVER SEEN A COMPASS SPIN LIKE THAT BEFORE!

IT LOOKS LIKE WE'VE GOT A COMPLETE ELECTRONIC DRAIN. CHECK THE GENERATORS.

CAP, NONE OF THE ELECTRONICS ARE WORKING.

THE GENERATORS ARE RUNNING, BUT THEY AREN'T PRODUCING ANY ELECTRICITY.

CAPTAIN HENRY GOES ON DECK.

HUH? THE SKY... THE SEA... IT'S ALL BLENDED TOGETHER. THERE'S NO HORIZON.

THE SEA... IT'S LIKE A MILKY FOAM ALL OVER.

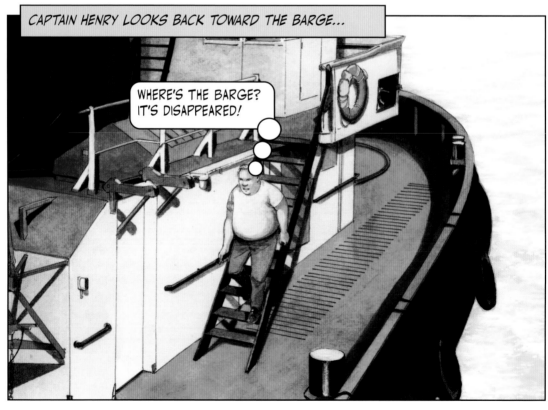

CAPTAIN HENRY LOOKS BACK TOWARD THE BARGE...

WHERE'S THE BARGE? IT'S DISAPPEARED!

CAPTAIN HENRY HEADS BACK TO THE BRIDGE.

HOLD ON, EVERYONE. I'M GOING TO PUT HER INTO FULL AHEAD!

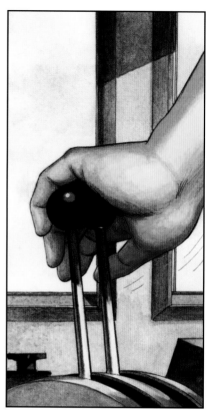

IT FEELS LIKE SOMETHING IS PULLING US BACK. COME ON, BABY!

ROARRRR

GRADUALLY, THE TUG MAKES HEADWAY, AND THE CREW BEGINS TO SEE THE HORIZON AGAIN AS THEY CLEAR THE STRANGE FOG.

LOOK, CAP, THE ELECTRONICS ARE WORKING AGAIN.

TAKE THE WHEEL. I'M GOING TO CHECK OUTSIDE.

WHEN CAPTAIN HENRY LOOKS BACK, HE CAN SEE THE BARGE CLEARLY.

I CAN SEE THE SKY, AND THE SEA IS NORMAL AGAIN.

LET'S KEEP HER GOING. PHEW! THAT WAS A CLOSE CALL.

THE GOOD NEWS MADE IT TO MIAMI WITHOUT ANY FURTHER PROBLEMS. LATER, CAPTAIN HENRY FOUND A WHOLE BOX OF NEW BATTERIES STORED ON BOARD THAT HAD MYSTERIOUSLY LOST THEIR CHARGE AND WERE COMPLETELY USELESS.

THE END

43

FACT OR FICTION?

More than 100 planes have disappeared and countless boats have gone missing in The Bermuda Triangle. Could all of these disasters have occurred in this area just by coincidence? Or might this spooky place be cursed by supernatural forces? Maybe we will never know. Here are some of the arguments.

UNSOLVED MYSTERIES

There have been many search and rescue attempts by the Coast Guard in The Bermuda Triangle area that have turned up no evidence of an accident. This is very unusual for plane crashes or shipwrecks at sea. This is most notable in the case of Flight 19 (see page 20).

There have been many cases of disappearances in which lengthy investigations by government panels have been unable to learn what happened to the ships or planes. They have been forced to declare these cases unsolved mysteries.

There exist recordings and written statements of encounters with UFOs, made by pilots flying in The Bermuda Triangle. The recorded voice of the pilot, José Torres, in 1980 is a good example.

There are even first-hand accounts from the people lucky enough to have survived what seem to be supernatural events, such as Captain Don Henry (see page 38).

or natural?

A HARSH AND UNPREDICTABLE ENVIRONMENT

The environment of the Mid-Atlantic area is extremely dangerous. There are fast-running currents, which can carry wreckage far away from a crash site. In the case of Flight 19, the Avengers were well known to be extremely heavy planes. If they crash-landed in the ocean, there was little chance of them floating for long, if at all.

The U.S. Coast Guard believe that a combination of harsh conditions, and human and mechanical failure are to blame. The area is also subject to sudden storms and tornadoes at sea, (called waterspouts) which can prove disastrous.

The Navy's Project Magnet studies magnetic forces around the world. It has passed over the area many times and has not found any unusual magnetic disturbances.

Wrecks litter the coastline

GLOSSARY

altitude Height in the air, measured in feet or metres.

barge A type of boat used mainly for carrying goods. Often it is towed through water by another boat.

bridge Area on a ship where the navigation controls are.

cargo Goods carried by a boat, plane, or other vehicle.

compass Magnetic needle used for navigation that indicates the direction a ship or plane is travelling.

derelict When something has been abandoned, particularly a ship at sea that has been deserted by its captain and crew.

frequency Number of times per minute that energy, such as a sound wave, spins round and back in the opposite direction again. People use the same frequency to communicate using a radio.

galley The name of a ship's kitchen.

generator Machine that changes energy into electricity. It provides the power on a ship or plane.

horizon Line where the sea appears to meet the sky.

interference Fuzzy sound from a radio that occurs when two sound waves meet each other.

lightship Ship with very bright lights anchored at dangerous spots to help prevent accidents.

mast Tall pole that holds up a ship's sail.

navigation Steering or directing, particularly of a boat or a plane.

peninsula An area of land almost completely surrounded by water but connected to a larger mass of land.

poop deck Small area at the back of a ship that is higher than the main deck.

port Place where ships can pick up or unload cargo.

radar Screen that uses radio waves to detect objects.

ruddy Reddish skin colour.

rum runner A person, or a boat, carrying illegal alcohol.

schooner Type of ship that has a main mast in the center and a smaller one in front.

shoals A shallow place in water created by a bank of sand.

steamer Ship powered by an engine that burns coal. The burning coal produces smoke (steam) that comes out of a boat's chimney.

tolerable Something a person will put up with, but does not like.

tow-rope Long, strong piece of rope used to pull something along.

transmission Messages sent and received by radio waves.

twenty-four hour military time When the hours in a day are shown by numbers 0-24, instead of 0-12. Military time starts at midnight, so what we call 3:00p.m. is 1500 hours in military time.

FOR MORE INFORMATION

FOR FURTHER READING
If you liked this book, you might also want to try:

Bermuda Triangle
by Andrew Donkin, DK 2000

The Disappearance of Flight 19
by Lawrence David Kusche, Harpercollins 1980

The Mystery of The Bermuda Triangle
by Chris Oxlade and Anita Ganeri, Heinemann Library 2000

UFOs: Alien Abductions and Close Encounters
by Gary Jeffrey, Book House 2006

The Bermuda Triangle
by Nathan Aaseng, Lucent Books 2000

The Bermuda Triangle: Opposing Viewpoints
by Norma Gaffron, Greenhaven Press 1994

Guide to the Unexplained
by J. Levy, DK 2000

INDEX

Web Sites

Due to the changing nature of Internet links, the Salariya Book Company has developed an online list of Web sites related to the subject of this book. This site is updated regularly. Please use this link to access the list:

http://www.book-house.co.uk/grmy/berm